My Still Waters

An Anthology of Self-Hope

Edited By:
Austie M. Baird

A.B.Baird Publishing
66548 Highway 203
La Grande OR, 97850
USA

www.abbairdpublishing.com

Competition Winners

My Still Waters: An Anthology of Self-Hope was born in a large part out of a writing competition held by A.B.Baird Publishing – these are the winners of that competition.

Grand Prize:
An Unlearning
By Melissa Felson
@intotheminefields

Runner Up:
Advice for Little Me
By Linda Lokhee
@lindalokheeauthor

People's Choice:
Making Sense of This Shape
By Itchy Brained
@itchybrained

We wish to give a sincere thank you to all who participated in this writing competition or voted in the peoples choice, without your continued support and faith in us we would not be able to do the things that we do.
Thank you!

Table of Contents

A Stone or a Rose   p. 1

Advice for Little Me   p. 2-3

Alike   p. 4

An Unlearning   p. 5-6

As We Grow   p. 7

Awakening   p. 8

Back to You   p. 9-10

Be Gentle   p. 11

Be the Light   p. 12

Beautiful   p. 13

Beauty in the Balance   p. 14

Becoming   p. 15

Befriending Otherness   p. 16

Beginning   p. 17

Bloom   p. 18

Blossom   p. 19

Blue   p. 20

Born for More   p. 21

Brave   p. 22

Broken is a Thing I have Met Before   p. 23

Butterfly   p. 24

Calling Strength   p. 25

Cipher   p. 26

Collage   p. 27

Comfort Zone   p. 28

Communion   p. 29

Conversations With My Reflection   p. 30

Cycle   p. 31

Cycles   p. 32
Detached   p. 33
Even Though   p. 34
Everlasting Imprint   p. 35
Faith   p. 36
Fighting Spirit   p. 37
Fixated   p. 38
Focus   p. 39
Free   p. 40
Free Falling   p. 41
Freedom   p. 42
From Darkness Into Light   p. 43
Future Generation   p. 44
Give & Take   p. 45
Growing Pains   p. 46
H.F.   p. 47
Happiness   p. 48
Her Prism's Palette   p. 49
Holding On   p. 50
Humility   p. 51
I Am My Own Refuge   p. 52
I Found Out I Have Anxiety Today   p. 53
Iconoclast   p. 54
I'm Worth my Crown   p. 55
In Order to Overcome Obstacles   p. 56
In the Darkness I Stand   p. 57-59
Inevitable   p. 60
Inheritance   p. 61
Insecurities   p. 62
Into the Minefields   p. 63

Just Like That   p. 64
Just What I Need   p. 65
Kindness   p. 66
Labyrinth   p. 67
Lashes   p. 68
Learning to Love Your Scars   p. 69
Lessons   p. 70
Library of Life   p. 71
Life's Storms   p. 72
Limitless   p. 73
Live Ferocious   p. 74
Lotus   p. 75
Make Room   p. 76
Making Sense of this Shape   p. 77-78
Midnight Garden   p. 79
Mirror, Mirror   p. 80
Moments   p. 81
Morning's Song   p. 82
Mosaic   p. 83
My Brand of Bravery   p. 84
My Broken Mind   p. 85
My Quest   p. 86
New Chapters   p. 87
Observe   p. 88
Of Love Divine   p. 89
One's State   p. 90
Owning Your Darkness   p. 91
Pieces of Me   p. 92
Polaris   p. 93
Return to Sender   p. 94

Revive My Growth	p. 95
Ribs Removed	p. 96-97
Ruin	p. 98
Self-Portrait Triptych	p. 99-101
Self Satisfied	p. 102-103
Shedding, Threading	p. 104
Silence	p. 105
Steady	p. 106
Strength	p. 107
Sugar Substitute	p. 108-109
Summer	p. 110
Sunday Morning Self-Actualization	p. 111
Suspended	p. 112
Tapestry	p. 113
Temperate Temptress Tempering Tempest	p. 114
That is Life	p. 115
The Cloak	p. 116
The Dance Never Ends	p. 117
The Feast	p. 118
The Fight	p. 119
The Stars' Healing Lullaby	p. 120
The Sticky Note Version	p. 121
The Sun's Plight	p. 122
This is What it Feels Like	p. 123
The Truth	p. 124
Therapy Thoughts	p. 125
Think Tank	p. 126
To Let Myself Go	p. 127
To You	p. 128
Unravel	p. 129
Wake the Beast	p. 130

Want Not   p. 131
Wear Your Battles Like a Crown   p. 132
Went on a Solo Trip to Mend My Heart   p. 133-135
When You're Gone   p. 136
Winter's Beach   p. 137
Winter's End   p. 138
Words I Wanted to Say   p. 139
Years of Untangling   p. 140-141

A Stone Or A Rose...

I shake and shed
the petals of grief.
Sometimes my soul is distant
and quiet.
My thoughts travel like
a river
or the wind,
constantly changing direction,
flowing this way and that,
silky strings of melancholy
like tall blades of grass.
They march on like car wheels
or the seasons
or life.
But sometimes my soul is
full of laughter,
of bouncing energy,
of sunlight
of maddening joy,
of hope,
like branches reaching higher,
like sunflowers meeting the warmth,
letting the sun kiss their faces.
I never know which days
my soul will awaken
a stone
or a rose.

Kimberly Olivera Lainez

Advice for Little Me...

Dear Young Me,

sweet and pure,
just four years old.
Here's some advice from the future,
to always be bold.

Board your Unicorn girl,
there's magical sights to behold.
This world's going to show you
that life is not a mould.
Feel your way around,
it's a multitude of colour.
Some days will be bright,
and others will be duller.

Listen;
to those that are wise.
Compassion;
be sure to sympathise.
Gratitude;
recognise and show it.
Live;
this life fully with no regret.
Love;
fiercely with a passion untold.
Accept;
not all things can be controlled.
Embrace;
mistakes are yours to learn.
Generosity;
share what you earn.
Speak;
your truth inside.

Trust;
the voice that guides.
Forgive; so you can be whole
Laugh;
every day as a goal.

Linda Lokhee

Alike...

maybe we are more alike
than I ever thought
yet on many levels
we are worlds apart
then again
we were never made
to carry the same heart

Lizzy in words

An Unlearning...

I used to think I needed to be loved and admired to be enough.

When I was seven, I learned that looking out for my brother meant that my grandparents would point out what a good big sister I am.

When I was nine, I learned that if I got up in the middle of the night and cleaned the house, it would make my mom happy and she would tell me how much she loves me.

When I was eleven, I learned that when a boy tells you to kiss him and you hesitate, he puts you in a headlock. I also learned that when you kiss said boy, it feels warm and fuzzy like I love you does.

When I was thirteen, I learned there was more warm and fuzzy where that came from —in a sixteen-year-old boy's bedroom when his parents weren't home. That is when I first learned to search for the feeling of I love you in a rough embrace.

When I was nineteen, I learned that it's easier to spend four years with constant "I love you's," even when they don't quite reach your heart, because it's safer than letting it go and the risk of never getting it back.

Then, when I was twenty-one, and warm fuzzy feelings from boys who took more than they gave had left me empty, it was then that I first began to learn that the most important "I love you's" don't come from grandmas or moms or boys whose lips make you feel on fire.

And when I was twenty-three, I said I love you to myself and, for the first time, I meant it.

I've said it every day since.

Tomorrow, I will be twenty-four.

What will I learn next?

Melissa Felson

As We Grew...

I sense peace.
More often, more frequently.
And yet, I still learn to ease my mind.
Stop circling thoughts in my head,
That get louder and louder.

It seems that I still feel the nagging
Sound right beside my chest.
This time not as a longing in far distance,
But as a crystal clear beat.
It is my true north calling me,
Attracting me like a magnet.
Arriving as a melody
That I can play.

I pause here and now,
Sensing my breath,
And acknowledge the moment.
Feeling the gratitude wandering
Along my arms,
Settling in my heart
Into a new home.

I write to find peace,
When the world is out of order.
I believe in hope
And in small steps.

Imagine the North wind appearing
As a breeze,
Calling you.
As you wander in tiny steps towards it.

Miriam Otto

Awakening...

Your inner voice confounded
in the ricochet off the asphalt.
Draped in steel
and reinforced concrete,
we eroded the synchronicity:
of bone with earth,
flesh with the oceans,
sinew with fire,
and equanimity with air.
The only recourse left, to
dive head first into rude awakening.
Swim amongst sharks
mobilized by the scent of fear,
allowing their teeth to impale
years of conditioning,
culpable of removing you from yourself.
The blood of generations
oozing from your body,
releasing your heart
to pirouette on the precipice
of its fall from grace
wringing traditions outworn,
for your soul to be reborn.

Ambica Gossain

Back to you...

I wondered why I'd lost you
but I realized I was the one giving up
I lost your essence and your meaning
emotions running high
I'm sorry I gave up on you
you stuck around, in silence waiting
until I saw the light
the light you and I used to make shine so bright

you've always been my strength
but I was the one who made you weak
thinking you'd forsaken me

you only waited patiently
I see it now, I need you like the air I breathe
you flow through me,
and I lost the way to set you free
my most precious gift, through which my feelings flow

forgive me for I love you
you are what God has given me
we'll start from scratch, just you and I
now my dear I see, by forsaking you, I've been forsaking me
I'll start again from the beginning, born out of my heart
the way it used to be
no obligated task, but raw emotion, purity
that's how you've always helped me cope
not to lose my sanity

and oh my dear I came so close
to losing that last spark of hope
but God reached down and touched my soul
oh darling how I missed you so
it will take time, the road is long, I'll stumble and I'll fall
I'll get back up and time will teach, just as long as I try
so if you can forgive me, give me another chance
then we will get to know each other all over again

and you will help me cope and breathe
through all the hardship life is giving me
and I will let you shine so bright
as God intended, you and I

Lizzy in words

Be Gentle...

Easy does it now
Your bruised heart needs time
Softly now
Go gentle on yourself
Healing isn't easy

Trust your strength
And that fighting spirit
to get you through

Nicole Carlyon

Be the light...

My world is vibrant colour
Interspersed with dark hues
After every violent storm
The light will always filter through

Nicole Carlyon

Beautiful...

Beautiful blossoms
emerge from
springtime branches
Me
taking chances
Vibrant life
emerging from
dormancy
Hope springs new
Beautiful you

Victoria Oliver

Beauty in the Balance...

At 17 I plucked myself from my eyebrows.
Grandma said to be careful because
they wouldn't grow back, but I held
the tweezers eagerly
because none of the girls were as hairy
as I was and I was too young
to see beauty in the mosaic.
Each tug bit the tear duct
but I was always one more away
from almost good enough, chasing symmetry
in waning rainbows that I later filled
with blunted crayon and
sharpened memories.
Today, it is not the arch I seek,
but the fulcrum between reflection
and want. Wisdom is knowing
what you have and what you do not have
are both soil for contentment.

Gina Sares

Becoming...

I am finally free
Unchained and unbound
By the changes happening inside
Feeling the release of gravity
Floating along the stream
I am becoming
One with the dream
Floating along the stream
Feeling the release of gravity
By the changes happening inside
Unchained and unbound
I am finally free.

Angela Marie Niemiec

Befriending Otherness...

Take otherness
out of your pocket.
Lift it to your heartbeat
to remind it that it, too,
has a mother.
Feed it sunlight and kisses
until it grows to true size,
then shape it into a staff.
See how it lengthens your gait,
steadies your steps like
the arm of a friend?
Now, raise it to the heavens
with thanks and behold
the splitting sea.

Gina Sares

Beginning...

I shake
and shed
the flower of my sorrow
ready for tomorrow.
I open my palm
and let the seeds
fly into the wind,
hopeful for a
new beginning.

Kimberly Olivera Lainez

Bloom...

Plant the seeds of hope
Water my soul
And watch me bloom

Nicole Carlyon

Blossom...

Sit in quiet contemplation
and watch in awe
As the truth of your soul
Unravels and unfolds
Like a beautiful flower
Blossom my darling
Bloom

Nicole Carlyon

Blue...

on the days she felt blue,
she closed her eyes and imagined
the cloudless sky
that reached forward forever
and the sound of the ocean,
a rhythmic lullaby for her tired soul
and a calmness reached into
her mind and whispered the
song of the bluebird
come home to rest

Linda Lokhee

Born for more...

The girl I used to be screams at me from across a crowded room
Beckoning me to part the sea of unfamiliar faces
Return to my dreams
I forge my way through
Head held high
Deep down I know I was born for more

Nicole Carlyon

Brave...

carry a brave heart
for when this world crumbles
bravery is required
to carry out kindness and compassion

Lizzy in words

Broken is a Thing I've Met Before...

Broken is a thing I've met before.
In the lines of his tattoo that I used to trace,
In the gap between his teeth
just small enough to be sweet,
In the playfulness of his bright blue eyes
and his dusty blonde cropped hair.
But never.
Did I think.
We'd meet again.
In you.

Broken is a knife who's blade I've felt
and lived to tell the tale.

Broken is a monster
in whose snarling face I've laughed.

Broken is a villain I'd thought I'd slain
at last, in you.

Good thing I kept my sword.

Melissa Felson

Butterfly...

My predisposed demeanor of alchemy envelops my destiny
without choice, this questionable stage of my existence I did not ask
for.
No sight of understanding I've gained yet on this process of life,
but blindly and bravely, I continue to believe in its goodness.

The unknowing of such awe look not at me twice-
Easily dismissed I am as ordinary,
but the journey ahead tugs at my optimistic nature.

There's an ineffable magic I keep but know not where it will take
me,
I trade my trepidation for patience and find comfort in whispers of
intuition.
My dreamy state offers subduction and collects my energy as toll,
without a glimmer of attention except for my own,
I become friends with my spirit.

Encased in darkness but incredibly aware, I realize it is only by eye
that others first detect change.
No transparency surrounds me as the hard work of solitude carries
on-
Fervently protecting the un-veil with due time.

And effortlessly one day like waking from a long abstraction,
I was me on the outside now, as my heart beauty-fully unfolded on
my sleeves.

Geninne

Calling Strength...

The mountains call to me
stand strong
The valleys echoing
endure long
History beckoning
hold on
Don't give up

Don't give in

Don't be afraid

to begin again
Calling strength
from up above
Calling strength
from those I love
Calling strength
from deep within
I listen long
and rise again

Victoria Oliver

Cipher...

My eyes, the sieve
As I sit between
No melancholy
But my own
All the while
Deciphering everything
Or so I'd like to think-
Analytical images flicker
Like Morse code
And voices jump around
In all the fleeting spaces
Of this mind
Loud and soft
On a fading disk
And in the tiny crammed space
I cling to remember
To self-love, respect

Greg Oman

Collage...

Things Fall Apart.
The problem is
That's how we usually leave them—
In pieces,
While we walk away shaking our heads
Or licking our wounds
Or holding our hearts.
But what if we lifted the brittle bits
And pieced them back together—
A golden kintsugi collage
To create something new and beautiful
Out of what was broken
In our lives.

Garrett Ashe

Comfortzone...

She listens to her heart beat.
20 steps or less are needed to reach her goal.
But she decides to go into another direction.
Keep your heart open, she whispers,
trusting in the vast land of the new
like a void that opens up when you pass the gate
of decisions.
Standing at a turning point,
like we all did
once or many times,
with the possibility to grow even more.

We enter a black space called the new.
With many opportunities,
not knowing what to expect.
There is no left or right.
No bottom or top.
The rules are different here.

She stretches her comfort zone,
bends her arms over the left side,
and then far away into the air.
She is ready.
She pauses and breathes,
stumbles, jumps, runs,
  goes back to slow motion,
rests, breathes again with a deep inhale
and then looks in surprise back.
She already made it.

Miriam Otto

Communion...

Finally, at peace
(A life outside the chaos)
She manifested communion with her soul

Nicole Carlyon

Conversations With My Reflection...

I sit face to face with the girl in the mirror each day. My hands press against the smudged glass barricading us from each other. Her green eyes staring back at mine as tangled brown hair falls over her bare shoulders. Most mornings we say nothing as we gaze over one another. And I can't help but wonder what goes through her mind as she stares back at me. Does she recognize the person on the other side? Or is my image merely a distorted reflection of a girl she used to be?

Maybe she wonders when it all started. Wondering when the little girl who used to smile ear to ear and press her face against the mirror to see through disappeared. Why tank-tops and shorts were swapped out for oversized sweaters and adolescent shame. Why she began hiding the freckles on her sun-kissed face with paint. How she doesn't believe it when people call her beautiful anymore.

Does she whisper affirmations each morning through the glass the way I do? About how today we will love ourselves. Today we will change. Today we will be happy. Today we are beautiful. Does she believe them? I hope so.

This morning I sat face to face with the girl in the mirror. Our feet almost touching as I spread my legs across the bathroom floor staring at her, tangled brown hair falling over my shoulders. And I told her that I am learning. I am learning that my body is not a public exhibition of flaws for others. That I am more than unwelcomed stares on the subway and a lingering embrace. That I will no longer use my skin as a canvas for others to paint over in the search of self-validation. That I am not a number which fluctuates every other month. That I understand the battles she's faced, and she's come out stronger than I could have imagined. That I am not there yet, but there is a thin line between healing and healed and I am still learning how to be enough. And that is okay.

Elizabeth Todoroska

Cycle...

Cycle
every day we can grow
not in size but in light
it seems we might rise slow
but every step leads us right
to the source of unlimited
flow

Cyra Felber

Cycles...

Learning,
    unlearning,
        relearning,
unlearning,
    relearning,
        eternal
            cycle,

like the barber pole that
spins on the corner of
the square, in the town
I try to forget.

Learning to love,
taught incorrectly,
learning to trust,
taught deceit,
learning to dream,
taught harsh reality,

removing the source, that
powers the cylindrical spin,
today I break the cycle, and
relearn one final time.

Jason Whitt

Detached...

Her reality is where she clings
not to made up fairy tales of kings,
echoing across the airwaves
transmitting a message of tenacity.

Onward, never giving up
and never giving in,
electric shockwaves soaring
guiding effervescently
through fiber optic skin.

With ferocious strength
she sees through the wires
where truth rises above all pain
and passion ignites her inner fire.

Ascending with urgency to the top
over maniacal onlookers,
assuming a fictitious doom,
she's cast them from her life,
for negativity she keeps no room.

Eyes wide open
and wings to match,
breaking free from all cages
and from tethers
now detached.

Angela Marie Niemiec

Even Though...

my body can breathe
even though I'm tired
inhale strength
exhale defeat
 breathe
soak in peace
release doubt
welcome rest
dispel stress
my body is a gift
I will respect its limits
wisdom:
when to push forward
when to lay back
success is not always had
in the striving
but in the belonging, crying
sighing, beholding, resting, trusting
believing, being

Victoria Oliver

Everlasting Imprints...

I am the needle
piercing through the dark sheath
pinpoints of light forming
welcoming the change.

I am the smoke clearing
waving fumes from the air
breathing away the toxicity
of psychological warfare.

I am the frequency
of high vibrational waves
rippling through the walls
drumming on your heart
and beating through each vein.

I am the gates of heaven
open wide and welcoming
the sound of your footsteps
as they leave an everlasting imprint
while walking away from the darkness.

Angela Marie Niemiec

Faith...

Hold steady my love
A journey of a thousand lifetimes
Does not rely on a single breath

Nicole Carlyon

Fighting Spirit...

Wild one
with the messy hair
And eyes that shine iridescent
Don't let them break you
Your spirit can move mountains

Nicole Carlyon

Fixated...

fixated by the future
while the world is
in the present
I live life
longing for tomorrow
not engaged in
the moments
I capture
today
today
I capture
the moments
not engaged in
longing for tomorrow
I live life
in the present
while the world is
fixated by the future

Jason Whitt

Focus...

focus more
on outshining yourself
than on outshining others

Lizzy in words

Free...

For the first time in forever
I felt like I was enough
Not for you
For me
Such a simple concept
But it set my soul free

Nicole Carlyon

Free falling...

I am my own inspiration
I drift
Weightless
I celebrate my victories
I accept my flaws
I am free falling
Into love with myself

Nicole Carlyon

Freedom...

For a lifetime
anger masked my fear
Today I let my guard down
Today the tears fell
Finally, pain
No longer numb
Today I begin

Nicole Carlyon

From Darkness into the Light...

Darkness I felt-
Nowhere to go, nothing to see.
Punished, by the few so-called members
of my extended family tree.
For 10 years, there I was, aching to be free.

I was bloodied and bruised,
Often the subject of their contempt and abuse.
"YOU ARE A LIAR AND NO ONE BELIEVIES YOU"
-they used to say.

I was. Indeed, I was, at war with myself,
A battle of angst, as one might say.
Whether to take a vow of silence and obey,
Or to fight and my snatch my light, my freedom away.

And I will be honest, for a long time, it was the former that I chose,
Probably out of fear, and partly out of hope;
That one day they shall have mercy,
and that would be the end of my woes.
But so naïve and wrong was I,
Forgot that monsters never stop, in fact they hanker for us to cry.

So, one day, I chose to fight,
Said to myself, 'at least, give it a try.'
So, I fought back hard that day,
And continued to do so, the next day and the day after.
As I fought, that darkness that had been lurking within me,
I could feel it no longer.

Yes, the fight was difficult,
it was scary and often felt like a dynamite.
But I am glad that I stood my ground, I am glad that I chose to fight,
Because this dear fight was my journey back into the light.

Sharmila Maitra

Future Generations...

I will dance here tonight beneath a blood red sky
Under the watchful eyes of my ancestors
Shed the skin of my past
As I crawl out from beneath the rubble of years of conditioning
I shall rise from the flames
Willing to fight for freedom and integrity

Nicole Carlyon

Give & Take...

I think we all
give parts
of ourselves
to others
we wish
they would
give back
to us

Lizzy in words

Growing Pains...

I am in a constant struggle between being honest with myself and
being kind with myself
I do not understand why I cannot do both
Why truth is synonymous with brutality
Untangle your necklaces from the lies you lull yourself to sleep with
There is so much more room for lovers when you stop sharing a
bed with your mistakes

Itchy Brained

H.F. ...

You carry me
in the palm of Your hand
catching me
before I even know I'm falling

leading me
in directions I wouldn't go on my own

protecting me
from what to me is unknown

teaching me
to trust the journey
that time is in Your hands
with You beside me there isn't a storm
that I could not withstand

Lizzy in words

Happiness...

Happiness
what's that feeling tickling under my skin?
was that a smile?
this autumn breeze smells like
back from hell
why am I here, where I always wanted to be
am I, am I allowed
 to be happy?

Cyra Felber

Her Prism's Palette...

She could only ever be herself
Not wired to be like anyone else
Electrically static she was
Automatic on driving her truth
Ingrained to the core of her deep soul
Not one to feel lightly or let go
Resolute that she would never quit
She could never be a hypocrite
No matter countless times life would fall
She did always believe through it all
Life could reprise the hurt in her eyes
But never touch the love in her soul
She was born with a depth in her core
A very old soul from years before
She believed in love for all mankind
Searching for the best that she could find
No matter what life would throw her way
She always did her best by each day
She owned her idiosyncrasies
Encaustically lived as she pleased
She used her own brush to paint her world
Her opulence refracting in swirls
The finest ever of wisdom pearls

Denise Rusley

Holding On…

Tiresome days of self-reflection
A grief of weeks
With seemingly no end
Bouncing thoughts
With no particular aim
Fighting a legion-
An enemy self made
And to proclaim it
Is to give it merit
Calling it into existence
With a waking eye
Realizing doubt and despair
Are merely brothers
And they will seep
And will supplant
If you turn the spout

Greg Oman

Humility...

He wasn't born on his knees;
But rather, he bent
Only as life humbled him.
For, as every babe finds,
We must first learn to crawl,
Before being blessed with the strength
To truly stand tall.

Garrett Ashe

I Am My Own Refuge...

I know you feel like we have nothing in common
That the language I speak is foreign
But don't you ask yourself why

Your tears seek my refuge to dry
Why your frantic heart slows
In the shade of my boughs
Why your restless soul roots
In my burgeoning shoots
Why your weary feet answer
My susurrations summons
Don't you recognize the whispers
As your own

Ambica Gossain

I Found Out I Have Anxiety Today...

I found out I have anxiety today.
This sentence is both fact and fiction to me.

How does one find out they have anxiety?

Can you really find something that has been there all along,

*Is the acknowledgement of a truth akin to Columbus-like
discovery?*

Hasn't anxiety gleamed in each shard of glass where I've sought
validation?

*Sat cross-legged in the middle of my chest like stone sunk to
riverbed?*

Has it not made me stranger amongst my closest friends

And permanent guard against phantom foes?

These ears,
Who have heard my silent shriek
So long it has dimmed to a dull throbbing in my temples,

They ring with the shrill siren of diagnosis,

Of a name to a fearful face.

I found out I have anxiety today.

This sentence is both fact and fiction,

Fear and freedom.

A name for a foe I have fought for so long,

She is almost friend.

Melissa Felson

Iconoclast

My words can go places
I dare not go
Can be scantily clad
in seductive allure
Can cringe with disapproval
 I m not permitted to show
Can dare to dream,
jurisdiction governed by my heart alone
Can learn self-love
amidst pedantic chiselling galore
Can look me in the eye unabashed
and not abhor,
the iconoclast claiming this life as their own.

Ambica Gossain

I'm Worth My Crown ...

Gone are the days
Where my head's not raised
And wonder fogs up my brain.

Now are the times
Where the sun rays shine
Where my smile is bright
And my crown is finally placed

Jesselyne Abel

In Order To Overcome Your Obstacles...

It was in the breaking
When they began to regain their power

You see,
Some days you need to allow yourself to crumble
To hold yourself extra tight
Whispering you deserved better

Because
In order to heal
Let yourself

Reopen the wounds
And bleed out the poison

Khalisa Jiwa Mawji

In The Darkness...

In the darkness I stand,
Silent and still,
Only the echoes of judgement and ridiculing
Whispers rustle through the trees,
They lean over to cage me in,
The stars and moon disappear under the blanket of the night sky,
I am a lost boy wandering alone,
Navigating through life's crashing waves,

Inside me grows a storm,
In this strange place I do not belong,
But I still hold on to rope of hope,
Following the trail of bread
Left behind by someone who's walked here before,

I pray for change,
I pray for the day I can say I am who I am,
For how long can this go on.

Walking in the darkness,
The wind snarls at my existence,
The trees overlook me,
Bearing down on my cold corpse,
Life is a heavy load,
The only way out,
Is to follow the yellow brick road,
We don't know what lies on the other side,

But they told me this is not a fairy tale,
We make our own wishes and dreams,
We do not need the worn out red shoes that go on our feet,
How far to the end,
I do not know,
I've become a young man,

Life's empty promises is what I carry,

My Still Waters

They fuel the storm inside of me,
A cyclone, whirlpool start to form,
Drowning my soul,
My heart is the ship which beats the rhythm of hope.

The mountain is steep,
Rocky and jagged,
Standing tall and proud,
My feet stand steady on the firm ground,
It's time to release the load that I bear,

I can't take them up with me,

Burdens of the past,
I leave them behind,
This is the change I need to make,
As I start to climb,
The wind that circles the mountains entrap me with in its grip,
The mountain starts to break up the rocks,
So that I slip and fall,
I hold on tight,
This is what life has prepared me for,
My ultimate obstacle,
The challenge I must defeat.

As I reach the top and climb to the flat surface of the peak,
I look over to the horizon,
The suns light starts to uncover the darkness,
The warm rays, warm up my cold body,
I sit on the edge as an old man,
Life threw everything at me,
But I overcame,
Life's actions made me feel worthless,

But up here I find my worth,
Life's words drowned me,

But up here the waters can't reach me.

The storm inside me is calm,
Inside me I have found my peace.

Bearded Writer

Inevitable...

Inevitable,
love, loss, longing; cycles bred
by the winds of change.

Jason Whitt

Inheritance...

I refuse to feel shame
For my fear and insecurity
Passed down to me by my mother
And her mothers before her

I will wear it like a badge
For it has stripped each of us raw,
Opened us up like budding roses

Striped us with war paint and wisdom
Taught us to rise against the darkest tides
Within ourselves

Try as you will
You cannot make me apologize
For carrying, like redemption,
The very weapons that once wounded me

This is my sacred alchemy
This is my brand of bravery
The likes of which you will never know

Melissa Felson

Insecurities...

she was tangled in insecurities
oblivious to the power she contained
lying dormant yet shining through
for those who knew her heart
until they'd be awakened

and she herself would see
no truth was ever found
in all that insecurity

Lizzy in words

Into the Minefields...

Into the minefields
We warriors go
To face our pain
And claim our souls

Melissa Felson

Just like that...

and suddenly
I knew
I never was not whole

Bianca van der Kamp

Just What I Need...

My past is gone forever I am told
I am left with tracks embedded deep within my soul
Gifts of my past that I hold
Each jagged line
Each time I recall
Each memory it marks
Sometimes the scars are angry
Sometimes they scream
Sometimes the scars bleed
Sometimes they whisper
Sometimes the scars are just what I need
Each dream fades
Each time I awake
Each promise I embrace
My future is bright with unwritten chapters
A life forever He is sealing as my heart cries in the dark
I offer up my prayers on this journey of healing

Mark Wayne

Kindness...

if nothing else
be kind
so that His love
and grace
may shine
- through you -
upon others

Lizzy in words

Labyrinth...

With my right hand, I hold my heart, feeling its scars protrude into the flesh of my palm. Each scar serving a reminder of the purpose for the pen my left hand holds. Pen to paper, quite foolproof I think, this plan for a maze in which to hide this battered heart. But, a funny thing happens on the way to fabricate this multicursal puzzle. Recollecting the memories that beget the wounds these scars now cover, an epiphany is realized: why do I allow these scars to hold me in fear, hidden among a maze? So, underneath the sound of crumpling paper, a gateway opens, as my pen instead draws a labyrinth for searching this unicursal path, not with heart hidden, but with heart in hand.

Not all who are lost
want to be found, for peace is
found in the searching.

Jason Whitt

My Still Waters

Lashes...

Burrowing ugly bones between high
Voltage pylons
Arms have been rolled
Through sticker branch
Bundles
The scars
Stuck for keeps

I peel off layers I can no longer
Stomach
When
Suffering to persist
Beyond this printed composition bugs
       Am I more than the obvious

I grub through the layers
When
Restless for contentment
       Moreover
Wrenching tendons to stand and
Exceeding upper limits
Straining strings of events
And disentangling from
Old effort

The radiance of a former age
Hangs against
A network of thorns and
Spiral webs
Electrical circuits lean

      Focus on your own
      Personal confines
      I belong where I am
      Longing
      For lashes
         Flood the muted sky

Steve Zmijewski

Learning to love your scars...

Learn to love your scars
You keep hidden away
Buried like lost treasure
A thousand miles away

Learn to love your imperfections
You pick on day by day

Pinching and poking
At every little fault

Why do we pick on ourselves?
What good does it do
To peel off our layers
And feast on our flaws

Does it make us grow,
When we look in the mirror
Calling ourselves ugly
Expecting to bloom

Khalisa Jiwa Mawji

Lessons...

Wet was the light
the damp green earth glistening
the dirt sinking beneath shoes
slushy, muddy, liquid
the aftermath of a ritualistic cleansing.
Still, the flowers are singing
gulping silky water into their bodies,
teaching us in order to loom
we have to experience the rain first.

Kimberly Olivera Lainez

Library of Life...

Run with me
through this corridor of books,
each spine holding a different story,
a different memory
from the library of your life.
The pink blossom of first love,
the sting of jealousy,
of self-doubt,
of fear,
the blue ocean of heartbreak,
the week you thought you'd never recover.
Each time you stood up taller,
rising like the phoenix from the ashes.
Let me give you hope for the night,
a shard of sunlight in the dark.
Through each of life's seasons,
there has been a pattern of growth,
a blooming through the process,
a fresh breath of rebirth.
Look upon each intricate cover,
each book a moment in time,
each beautiful day
and each bad one,
displayed like paper cranes on a string.
There will always be better days coming.
Look upon this library wonder
and the blessing that is your life.

Kimberly Olivera Lainez

Life's storms...

Brace yourself
For life's inevitable storms

Face the destruction
Rise from the chaos
Reborn
Your multifaceted layers
Waiting to be explored

Nicole Carlyon

Limitless...

I am neither here nor there
Standing in the space between yesterday, today and tomorrow
Where the pain of the past cannot hurt me
Where the now will not define me
Where the future cannot consume me
I am limitless
I am free

Nicole Carlyon

Live Ferocious...

I used to tiptoe through life
Afraid of my own shadow
Not anymore
I will stomp and roar
Live ferociously
Look my demons in the eye
and laugh at their bewilderment

Nicole Carlyon

Lotus...

My heart opens like a lotus flower
Thick, thousand-year-old stems rise steadily from the river bottom

Pink bud peeking out above flat floating leaves
My heart is timid
Raised by roots of mud and muck,
It is taken aback by its own slow blooming,
Surprised by its own verdant self-actualization

My Vishnu heart, my heart of mire
Unstained, parts its petals
And gasps at its own great beauty
Not ornamental, but monumental

Learning to take up space
As it spreads itself wide
My lotus heart
Opens
My lotus heart
Blooms

Melissa Felson

Make Room...

Make room
In the womb of your life
For the unexpected
And rejoice in what you've been given
Right here
Right now
This breath is a miracle
These tears are cleansing somehow
And I'm standing with you
In love, believing
For your legs to hold you up
And wings to carry you
Right where you belong
Always carrying a song
Of hope
And surrender

Victoria Oliver

Making Sense of this Shape...

I used to keep a mirror in the same corner of my room as the one that we used for time outs. Always a place in my home for punishment. I would stand there every morning and watch myself get dressed. Taking in all of the accidents that my one day lover would see during our mornings together.

My mother made sure to install industrial strength light bulbs in every bathroom. Paying the highest price to find every flaw. Each hair that dared to show itself on my skin to be cited as an example of my many biological mistakes. Every unemptied follicle screaming how this body was utterly wrong.

In history class, I had only ever seen men doing the conquering and the claiming. I remember learning about exploration as an invasive thing. Space was never earned, only taken- ripped from the hands of others. Gentle fingers exploring my figure would be cut off for touching myself with too much tenderness. I could not justify becoming the Christopher Columbus of my own body- taking space so violently. So instead I shrunk back. Waved a white flag instead of my own. There was no kindness in their conquering, but I had no idea that there was no kindness in my surrender either.

In high school I would spend bus rides covering myself in paints and dyes I could not name. I didn't care, as long as it hid the fact that I was angry. Aging. Smiling. Living. I would eat more words than food on my plate, then smile and tell the world that my heart was full.

That is the thing about shrinking- it does not happen in isolation. My doctor explained that spot reduction is a myth- So as my skin shrunk tighter around itself so did my heart- Becoming smaller and smaller. Making myself feel less so I could stay in this tiny existence. Self-love is sometimes too heavy a load.

I wanted everything smaller- smaller wrists, smaller brows, smaller thoughts. I did not learn that expansion was another word for growth- could not wrap my head around what a privilege it is to exist in this world. I am walking taller now that I've taken my heels off. Found more color in my cheeks than any compact could ever promise. One day I was tired of feeling trapped, so I unbuttoned the top button of my smallest pair of jeans, and all of the confidence spilled out.

Whoever lied to you did so because they are afraid of you. Never forget that.

Itchy Brained

Midnight Garden...

my soul's in a tailspin
tears of blood
falling into the mud
where I wish
my memories would stay
but where would I be
without the pain
can I find the strength
to embrace
the thorns
growing from these roses
in my midnight garden

Victoria Oliver

Mirror, Mirror...

I ate myself alive that night
All fingernails and self esteem

I never knew why it unsettled me
Maybe because his gentle made me feel sharp
I was not used to being blade
He made my periods into question marks
My mirrors misleading
And it wasn't that she was a liar

She just made the truth seem so ugly
You can look at a flower through broken glass
And still be looking at a flower
Just mangled and chopped now

I am learning to not need their words
I am learning to feel my reflection instead of see it

Itchy Brained

Moments...

Time's always moving
never keeping still
Just like the words
flowing from my quill

I write to entertain
also to educate
I write for voices lost
To be an advocate
I write my feelings
to truly communicate
I write my magic
stories to imaginate
I write to learn
my mind will illuminate
I write to discuss
topics to articulate

I write to break the walls
inside that incarcerate
I write for so many reasons

I write to liberate

Linda Lokhee

Morning's Song...

On mornings when
Your heart awakens to the dawn,
Keeping beat in perfect time with the universe,
And your soul seems to vibrate with the very rhythm of inception,
You come to realize that you are immortal
In this sunbathed song of first light;
And God has etched the lyrics
In everything that is
For anyone who listens.

Garrett Ashe

Mosaic...

Just because I am broken
Doesn't mean you have to fix me

Mosaics are shattered pieces of glass
And yet they are breathtaking works of art

Nicole Carlyon

My Broken Mind...

A house hangs in the air
The winds now silent and still
Broken memories lie scattered across the floor
In a dark corner midst the chaos I sit
Tired and torn
Battered and worn
Forgotten and forlorn
Refreshed and serene
Rescued and clean
Loved and seen
Praying for forgiveness and mercy
I no longer see ghosts haunting the empty halls
The voices silent in my broken mind
A house now a home

Mark Wayne

My Quest...

I sail across the sky
treading lightly over the clouds.
The blossoms start to bloom
as spring arrives.
 I land on the crunchy grass
and I run.
I run towards a better future
rather than looking back on what has gone.
There will always be
bumps in the road
but looking back will never work.
For I want to live
as free as the birds that sing to me
as I pass.
Forever at one with nature.

Amy Littleford

New Chapters...

Midst the birth of spring
The fires of summer
The stars of autumn
The death of winter
I believe in magic and the deep mystery
of love, romance, and adventure.
I believe in healing and grace unveiled
of hope, restoration, and transcendence.
I believe in dreams and holy revelations
of the pain, sorrows, and shadows.
I believe in light and not fearing
of death, destruction, and darkness.
I believe in firsts and new beginnings
of heaven, salvation, and eternity.
Midst the birth of spring
The fires of summer
The stars of autumn
The death of winter

Mark Wayne

Observe...

What our ears heard
and our eyes saw
cannot be forgotten
but
our minds must forgive
the hurt and the anger
to move forward
for soul's healing

Linda Lokhee

Of Love Divine...

Dear body,
I'm sorry I did not
cleanse my palate
with gratitude
before meeting you
at the mirror.
I kissed the world
and spoke to you
with venom-soaked lips.
Today, I greet you
as earth greets
sky, seeing
water and warmth
and window
to heaven.
You are dance
of my soul,
a lesson in motion,
both host and guest
of Love divine.

Gina Sares

One's Stare...

I have a love
Or lack thereof
Of the person before me.

I stare at my coffee colored eyes,
An entrance to all emotions and my soul.
I stare at my full lips,
A pathway for words to be music to ones ear
I stare at my deep copper tone skin,
A beauty so bright its imitated by others

I have a love
Or lack thereof
Of the person before me.

I stare at my scars
Healed wounds that are simply reminders of my failures
Stare at my mistakes, short comings, empty promises.

I stare,
Even though mama says not to
I stare.

I stare,
In love with the person before me.
With everything she lacks
With everything she has
For she is beauty in the eyes of her Maker.

Jesselyne Abel

Owning Your Darkness...

Perhaps the most beautiful thing
about the darkness
Is its inability to be broken
by anything other than
the piercing rays of the sun.

Ambica Gossain

Pieces of Me...

pieces
of me
collected them all
diving and digging deep
carefully
put them back together
now I am
a beautiful
kaleidoscope

Bianca van der Kamp

Polaris...

You show me each and every day
that beauty can come from madness
and happiness can grow out of sadness
I see now what You want from me
the road I need to take
to let it go and let You lead
my feet are Yours to guide
as You do my heart and soul
my everlasting light

Lizzy in words

Relief...

When you feel the breeze kiss your face
And the birds in the wind sing their song
For a moment you believe nothing can go wrong
And you slow down your clumsy hurried pace
Cocooned by the sheer awesomeness
Of something greater than you
You can in that moment forget and choose to believe
God only burdens you with what you can relieve

Ambica Gossain

Return To Sender...

boxing up those fears
can't feed them any longer

I realize now
they were never mine to keep
you'll take care of them, won't you

Bianca van der Kamp

Revive My Growth...

I was a bag
Of mixed emotions
Disguised as smiles and laughter
That suppressed my inner demons
Whose hyena like voice chuckled
At my misery.

A bag of mixed emotions
That was shown through my timidity
While silent tears hit the floor
Cleaning my soul
Washing away the pain
Reviving my growth

Jesselyne Abel

Ribs Removed...

Watch me wash in warm waters, unwoven
born again in revelations of ribs removed
no longer confined, captured, or stolen
rid my body of bars and the particular prison
they're promised to prove
for my heart wears wings which feather my feet
in thrones of furious thunder
this throat will float on the echoes of bruised
and broken skies
a voice to bring breath to those buried under
dirt that drips like death from the damned,
how they salivate at the sound of their lies
deaf to the desecration, those words we endure
that bring bombs or demand our deflation
my skin, both above and within, once freckled
with ruin
the trembling tally of sins
every cut, every scar,
every moment I begged for white flags to blanket
my arms
when their ropes hung me in hurt, I cried as I cut
the thread with self-harm
I've stood on ledges
I've burned bitterly on the bridge's edges
only to find my own mind still has ink yet
to swim
and these rivers may wrap my song in their waves
but light on the surface shines from my rays
a harmony of hope held on high in my hymns
the beat of my soul does not belong
in a cage
bones break under blazing blood's weight
bright is the sight of a night flamed to light
that fire, a pyre of page

I finally drink my desires, as doubters swallow
and hollow my rage
this love I feel for me
is the loudest amplifier
glowing in the knowing of a new golden
age.

Molly Gentzsch

Ruin...

new life
will blossom
upon ruins

Bianca van der Kamp

Self-Portrait Triptych...

      I. Post-Breakup (June)

sitting in the empty tub, i face my warped reflection in the narrow faucet like a tête-à-tête business meeting. i hold the spouting showerhead like a watering can over my garden, goose bumps fading in patches of skin like desert rain. i watch droplets bounce off my spike-hairy legs, then slip down the drain. i turn the fountain towards my open mouth like a kid at a dentist, wanting to rinse out the night's sugar-sick residue (long island ice tea, white wine, sangria, and skittles) but the pressure tickles my lips—the crest of giggles i automatically suppress in my throat launches innocence and youth up from dusty depths, they embark into the ocean of my mind—sickening me more. i trace ripe aubergine bruises on my pale skin, evidence of my new roller-skates *(how much more money can be poured into distraction?)* i savor the pleasure of anticipated pain, but it makes me miss his drummer-hands around my neck in dim lights. i look at my body with objective, distant, interest; the way that, when you're depressed, you look at a molding block of cheese before you place it back in the refrigerator *(how much worse can it get).* i remember, years ago, sitting in this same useless position—neither a bath nor a shower—when my biggest concerns were loneliness and critiquing the lack of straight lines in my silhouette. i would guide the showerhead up and down my thighs, wishing it was a magic marker: revealing happiness in the form of a thigh gap. i am still lonely. but I have loved since then, and been loved *(am still loved?).* the break from ever-present loneliness was pure relief, addictive and fulfilling. i haven't lost that love, but i don't have him anymore: an emptiness that aches consistently and dully— baritone resonance that sets my sugar-coated teeth on edge. i close my eyes and move the showerhead slowly: up my thigh, over the crest of my belly, across my collarbone, over my shoulder, and finally down my back... imagining the warm pressure to be a human hand— his hand? no.

at least i like my curves now. i re-assure myself that i did get to that point on my own— before he ever squeezed me, before my body ever molded itself into his grip like we were meant to be, before his hands were ever full of me.

II. Punished for Backsliding (July)
the night i texted him for the last time
(for real), i slid into scalding water.
hands full with a gifted bath bomb
and a cold glass, white wine overflowing—
clinging to self-care like a baby
blanket. sweat mixing with steam,
i sang heartbreak songs to my empty
home. succumbing entirely to deep
pain, i let it swallow me whole, sliding
down until my hair floated around me.

a couple days have passed,
and i'm screaming. emotional distress
buzzes in the background, unnoticed—
overshadowed by the physical agony
of a burning yeast infection. naked
on the bed, where just a few nights ago
he had made me
feel sexy and powerful, now
i'm alone and whimpering and moaning
in ugly, humiliating despair. i writhe,
a hatred pulsing out of me for everything
in the vicinity. my vision is red-hot
as i spread my legs wide open, aching
to detach
from flesh, to float formless and free and far.

III. Looking in the Blurry Bathroom Mirror (August)
sometimes i wish he was still here—
only to feel how strong my legs

have grown. but
should a self-portrait be familiar?
where is the self, post-breakup?
or is it more visible now
than ever before.

Emily Neuharth

Self Satisfied...

Maybe I was trying to prove something. Piercing my nipples
like exclamation points for my being, consumed by the concept.
I'm accustomed to searching for affirmation in lovers' empty
eyes; I followed the male gaze to my chest. Now if they notice,
I wanted them to. Controlling my dark power peaks under a rosy
facade. Sensuality pulsing and encompassing like water or wind.

Yes, my Libra libido is an Air Sign— uncontainable like wind.
Identity-hungry, I compulsively collect labels. Even my nipples
have names: Stephanie (she's loud) and Susannah (she's rosy).
This felt like coming home, like finally understanding a concept
that came easily to others: loving my body. I only ever noticed
the differences, the marks, the bags, the jiggles; I longed to empty

out myself but that's an unreachable destination. Rather, empty
is a collective quality with ebbs and flows. Like how wind
can never be seen but its presence will always be noticed;
suddenly I wasn't scared of the needle. My sensitive nipples
have grown significant to my sexuality, as has pain. A concept
I quietly ponder, it's heavy but I like the power. Still, the rosy

hues linger in my wake relentlessly. But kindness is rosy,
I told myself... just like temptation, my tongue and empty
mouth. I sulk, soaking my infected piercings as these concepts
cloud my mind. The ten minute timer ticks slow, slower than wind
in humidity. Punished with swollen pus for licking my own nipples:
a shameful yet natural vice, my cock-eyed breasts finally noticed

and not criticized. With my neck curved like a sleeping swan, I notice
purpose and pleasure blooming like a prophesy fulfilled. I pinch 'til rosy
skies fill my lids while "At night, alone, I marry the bed."[1] My nipples
are royalty, proudly crowned by titanium barbells— never empty.
It was accidental self-discovery. All I need is one touch soft as wind

---

[1] Sexton, Anne. The Ballad of the Lonely Masturbator.

and I'm hard, hooked on the instant response. Addicted to the concept
of an innate sex-drive living both apart from and of me: that concept
alone is enough to arouse. I hope that others will bear witness and notice
my transformation. My flaccid confidence is resurrected; its tendrils wind
round my limbs, unfurling from my soft and hard chest. I reclaim rosy
as my own, and all of its connotations too. Somehow, I feel less empty.
Somehow, this inner-work churns. Somehow, because of my nipples.

I know these concepts will change as I do, but I will forever blush rosy
when the power of my body is noticed. And someday, I'll empty
my nipples for a baby, strong with a middle-name like Wind.

Emily Neuharth

Shedding, Threading...

amidst incessant pain
from unfolding and molting
overripening olden skin

there is ignescent gain
still unmolding and jolting
golden lightning from deep within

Swell Versed

Silence...

In silence I found myself
And in finding myself
I no longer fear the void

Nicole Carlyon

Steady...

Holding steady
Even with a spear
Through the heart
A miracle and a curse
With strange moments of clarity
Tempered by stranger dreams
While still awake
Distance-
The enemy of souls
Running around
Keeping busy
So that we forget
To touch and to hold
The things that are sacred

Greg Oman

Strength...

I don't measure your strength
by the weights you can lift
but by the road you have travelled
and how your heart and soul have handled it

Lizzy in words

Sugar-Substitute...

People keep telling me
I look amazing.
They beg:
tell us your secret.
what have you been doing?

I tell them:
I've made some changes to my diet.

I've stopped putting
external validation
in my morning coffee.

(sugar-substitute, highly processed
packaged sweetener
made of
artificial
Instagram likes and
bending over backwards like
acrobatics for attention;
blending myself into
you for approval
like stirring in your
favorite brand of
soy milk even though
soy makes me sick.)

I tell them
I opt for the real thing these days.
Organic
connection and
act natural, which is to say:
Don't act.
Be.

And, sure, it's hard to kick the habit and
I'm not perfect at it, but —
I tell them —
Life is much sweeter this way.

Melissa Felson

Summer...

Summer
there is a light
in her heart
that gleams and burns
and never returns
it burns bright
it burns wide
with delight
she is not afraid
in the cold
in the dark
in the wild
she is a child
who never lost herself
there will always be
summer's glare
in her soul

Cyra Felber

Sunday Morning Self-Actualization...

I ease into myself like a Sunday morning
Like the perfect pair of blue jeans and my ass is looking fine
I am a bath drawn bubbly, a charcoal sketch masterpiece
Smudged and blurry because no one can define me
I am the definition of self-love, self-like and all the phases in
between
Full moon on a starry night, I light up the sky like a solar flare

Flared nostrils when I'm angry, cause I'm allowed to be
Beautiful right down to the last drop of human, I go down smooth
Even that last bitter sip at the bottom
Cause you don't deserve my sweet without my salty

I am a celebration, and I will dance in the center of my own
spotlight
Till the lights go out and everybody goes home
And even then,
I will keep on spinning,
A planet needing no gravity, no adoring moon
In the light of my own sun
In the gravity of my own orbit

Melissa Felson

Suspended...

I am a mystery
even to
myself
like looking through
frosted glass
I begin
to second guess.

I am a performer
with a choice:
play to soothe
the whining critics
or a writhing inner voice.

I am a novel
half-read on the kitchen table,
a million endings
suspended in thin air.

Melissa Felson

Tapestry...

My healing is
a tapestry I
wrap myself in
on cold nights

Sewn by those
who have loved me
their steady hands,
my courage

Mother to my right
father to my left
all ready grip
and gentle touch

Friends and mentors
stitching bits of
security
that is to say

My healing is
a tapestry I
wrap myself in
on cold nights

And I,
with warmed soul
will ache
with gratitude

Melissa Felson

Temperate Temptress Tempering Tempest ...

i may have just enough
heliotropic treasure
to drain these inner rains

and perhaps enough tough
geostatic pressure
to tame these inward hurricanes

Swell Versed

That Is Life...

I've learned that it is best to equate life with an ocean,
Letting the moments greet you and pass you
Like the rising and falling waves.

As I lie here in this moment,
what use is it to me to worry over the waves to come,
lovely or monstrous as they may be?
Or to pine wistfully for the waves that have passed me?

All the while, paying little mind to the precious waves
breaking my shore on this day?
In this hour?

How can one possibly enjoy
their ocean foray
while continually oscillating
between past and future,
not ever relishing the experience
of the cool breeze on one's face,

the warm sand between one's submerged toes?

No, I shall not live this life as an observer,
forever looking forward and backward,
never placing my eyes on the pleasurable clay
beneath my feet.

No, not I.
From this day forward,
I do claim my ever small, ever vast right and role
as participant and actor, swimmer in this ever small and
ever vast
ocean
that is life.

Melissa Felson

The Cloak

Closing in
Shrinking days
Until it arrives
I don't want this

But maybe you did
Vivid seconds display
Your touch and your kiss
Are now neverwhere
A choice that darkness marinates
Do you now relish this anguish?
From the gathering
That will likely fall
On sunshine of our memory
Of you
For there was still love and light
To be felt

Greg Oman

The Dance Never Ends...

below the borders of salt
warmth flows in spirals
dancing with the ice cold waves
throwing order to the skies
competing with thunder and lightning
for the spoils of admiration

little do they know
their battles produce symphonies
calling to the masses:
the dance never ends
but the fight will turn to ocean currents
carving their place in you

Jasmine Barrett

The Feast...

I am sick of the glorified shrinking,
of sucking my stomach to slide between
waxed pages. Of making joy the fatted calf
so people can say I look great
when there's less of me. As if carved

clavicles were shelves
for compliments.
A cinched waist makes for shallowed breathing.
It is time to fill my lungs.
I will heed my body's wisdom and

feed my bones. Richness will drip from my
crimson lips and I will drink
from a sea of topaz. Wave after wave,
the salt will preserve me.
Satisfaction will be my measure.
I will no longer fold my frame into
a creaseless wad for wallets, cutting my arms
to be weighed like a bag of sand.
I will open wide, a volcano
broadening earth.
Every girl is now a daughter
I will teach to rip receipts that fall from lips,
to fight the collective waning
that weakens voice.
A growing generation
of widened wingspans and appetites
beyond beauty, listening to the world beneath
their skin and shifting the world
beneath their feet. Fearless of gravity,
yet taking their space
between the stars.
We will laugh with spoons in hand,
feasting on our wholeness.

Gina Sares

The Fight...

If you're running from the devil
then I believe you could win.
With the strength in your heart
and the spark in your eyes.
If you lose track of your thoughts
remember I am by your side.
A reminder
for you to stay alive.
He may promise you rest
but that is all lies.
He'll promise the world
hiding behind a disguise.
I am the truth
so cannot lie.
This road will be tough
but I promise you'll survive.
Don't look to the end
what's important is now.
Live, laugh and love,
that's all I can advise.

Amy Littleford...

The Stars' Healing Lullaby...

emerging from the shadows deep
i lie alone as moonlight seeps
an ache familiar fills my chest
returning, an unwelcome guest

though We are Past, love will still creep
emerging from the shadows deep
memories of our love remain
sweet blanketing to mask the pain

the stars outside begin to sing
notes of hope, enchantment will bring
emerging from the shadows deep
soft healing lullaby to sleep

glimmers flutter replacing dark
shoots a tiny happiness spark
inside my heart - a true faith leap
emerging from the shadows deep

Linda Lokhee

The Sticky Note Version I Crossed Over With Fading Ink...

I pause
A window witness
To days gone by and matters that cannot be fixed
Do not look down
      I said do not
      Look down
Or overhead
A cloudy sky pay no mind

Jarred wind and swallowed constraint
You are what I have
Tonight
 To dispense

Do not look down
      Do
      Not
      Look down
      I said

      Ahead

A purpose
Spans in stereo
Resounding gusts of change

  And I am wide awake
In your room
Waiting
On you

Steve Zmijewski

The Sun's Plight

The darkness that shrouded
 was just judgement clouded
 of a light so bright,
it blinded insight
of the sun s plight.

Ambica Gossain

This is What it Feels Like...

Summer finally receded
But the heat
Dulled the autumn foliage
As they hiked the trail
Upwards
She carried both
The life she imagined
The life they lost
The reckoning
Of which
Became heavier
As they hiked deeper
Into the wood
However
For the first time
She noticed
She no longer
Felt hollow

His memory is a blessing

Bonnie Shor

The truth...

the truth is
you
my darling
like a flower
are wonderfully made
created with a purpose
go out into the world
find it and share it with others
so that they as well
may bloom

Lizzy in words

Therapy Thoughts...

Tonight was the first time
in longer than I can remember
that I spent time with my mom
and felt like I could breathe.

In other words,
don't ever let anyone tell you therapy is a thing to be ashamed of.

Melissa Felson

Think Tank...

This conglomeration
Of unawares massed together
Sipping on the gossip
And not really yearning for a truth
But more so, glad for their happiness
Siphoning the warmth from each other's
Brow
Dancing intellects disperse their knowledge
Into the Ether, hopefully catching
Like the mist on a windowpane
Collecting
Until the flood restores some balance
Where mist becomes rain
Now falling on them
But unable to appreciate
The way a loving cloud can touch

Greg Oman

To Let Myself Go...

I had to let myself go.
I had to light the match
and burn all the bridges
of who I used to be
in order to become
who I was meant to be.
I had to shed and shed until
the raw and pink of my body
stood before God
and the sun and the sky.
It was in the wilderness
that I began to drop
the petals of shame,
of regret and loss
of self-righteousness and ego
of judgement and self-pity.
I let God seep into my bones.
I had to unravel
slowly
painfully
beautifully.
In every season
I had to stretch and sprout and grow
uncomfortable as it was
expanding expanding expanding
until I was blooming
a metamorphosis a journey a resurrection
body mind heart soul
the coming apart to come back whole
altogether new.
You see I had to let myself go
to find who I am.

Kimberly Olivera Lainez

To you...

the moment
you say yes
to yourself
is when you'll see
your life change

Lizzy in words

Unravel...

Falling apart for me is like breathing
To unravel
Is to become

Nicole Carlyon

Wake the Beast...

I tiptoe around afraid to wake the beast
He rests sleeping his power unreleased
Buried deep in the dark of my heart it begins
A dormant strength lies there within
I shake my head in utter disgust
At the emotions and uncontrolled lust
He laughs at my incessant crippling fear
As the only path lays before me so clear
I steal around the throne of my soul
As the imposters voice softly cajoles
If it is these moments that define my life
I must not shrink in the face of strife
I must continue for this is the time to fight
Believing from eternity there shines a light
For in this small dark place where he resides
I will go for his presence I cannot abide
I will arm myself with the sword of the spirit
Going forth confident and deliberate
To battle the enemy however arduous
In my heart where the beast lives in each of us

Mark Wayne

Want Not...

It's best to not want anything at all,
that way you won't face disappointment
when you are left empty-handed.
Joy is not found within things,
it is found in your heart.
Please just remember:
Happiness is
only found
within
you.

Angela Marie Niemiec

Wear your battles like a crown...

Being broken
Will never get you anywhere
But when you break
You soon begin too
Heal
And with healing
Comes rising

So never shy away
From the battles you've faced
&
The pain that soon followed

At the end of your journey
You can look back with admiration
That all this pain
Only made you far more
Stronger & wiser
Then ever before

Khalisa Jiwa Mawji

Went on a solo trip...

Went on a solo trip to mend my heart and I found...
It had been rejected, more than once,
Broken it was, shattered into a million pieces- My heart.
Thus, began the process of repair,
Trying to make whole of what was left of its aching parts.

Question: "What do people do to mentally and emotionally detach
themselves?"
Rejuvenate maybe? - I asked to myself.
Answer: "WANDER INTO WILDERNESS."
"*Well, if not the wilderness, then take perhaps a remote trip.*"- Said
the inner being.
And so, it began- The journey of reawakening.

Leg 1: Rendezvous with Sandur

"See Sandur in September." Mahatma Gandhi once said.
But folks, let me assure you, it is just as spectacular in October.
Beautifully authentic, like dewdrops sitting on a flowerbed.
The roads up the hills are curvy and calm,
And its monuments and temples have been spell-bounding millions,
with their relentless charm.

The Sandur hills once green now brown due to constant mining,
seem to send across a message.
And as I stood in front of it,
I felt that the mountains, to me, whispered through its gorgeous
wreckage -
"*Hey, look at me, years of pain and suffering visible on my body,
But here I still stand- Beautiful, majestic and strong.
For it is our hurt, our ache and our sorrow that evolves and re-
defines us;*

And it is our inner peace and happiness that helps us to continue our journey beauteous."

The hidden gem, which is the Shiva Vilas Palace of the princely state,
Reminded me of the leisurely practice called, 'Dolce far niente,'
As I enjoyed every moment the palatial beauty from sunrise till sunset.

There, in the handsome but shy town of Sandur,
I experienced first-hand, the beauty of being happy in solitude,
And the tranquillity of inner peace.
It was quite beautiful-my tryst with Sandur.

Final leg: A short date with Hampi

With mere hours left for my return,
I decided that the familiar and renowned Hampi also deserved a quick whirl.
Yes, of course, I visited monuments of the UNESCO's World Heritage Site,
And shopped at the Hampi Bazaar as well as bargained with all my might.

However, during my short stay at Hampi,
Something amazing happened.
Just a few kilometers from the so-called happening Hippie Island,
There is a Hanuman temple, seated atop the Anjaneyadri hill, like an unpolished diamond.
One needs to walk for almost a mile,
And then climb a massive 575 steps built in a non-traditional style.
At first, I thought; *'No way, I will not be able to do that.'*
But then something in me said - *'Just take one step at a time and do it with a smile.'*

And after twenty-five minutes, I not only stood at the whitewashed temple's ground,
But also got a magnificent bird's eye view of the paddy fields and the ancient ruins from the city around.

And as I stood there, mesmerized at nature's mysterious beauty,
Suddenly, I had a moment of astounding epiphany.

We always think that we cannot overcome our pain, sorrow,
Or anything that life might throw at us, in the name of obstacles.
But wrong we are, because every problem is solvable, every heart is mendable,
And every pain is treatable, only if we find the courage to move on to a brighter morrow.

And it was at that very moment when I realized,
If I can climb 575 steps and reach here, whilst neither giving up nor giving into my fear.
I can mend and heal what is broken inside.
All I have to do is take one step at a time and do it with a smile.
Thank you Hampi-For teaching me that.

I went on a solo trip to mend my heart,
And found that it is only I who can make myself happy,
Thereby, making self-love an important art.

Sharmila Maitra

When You're Gone...

I sat closest to the window,
looking out at the people below
and I saw you walking through the snow.
I could almost hear the crunch
under your boots
and feel the chill as your breath hit the air,
a cloud obscuring your face.
As you climbed the stairs, I braced myself, telling myself to be calm
and to keep breathing.
It was just a drink.
You sat down opposite me
I couldn't make up my mind how I should behave.
Maybe angry and hurt
because that was all I could feel for you?
But instead I smiled and asked you how you were.
We spoke about nothing important,
asking about people we didn't like.
You bought me a hot chocolate
as if to mend scares with a gesture
I stayed polite but reserved.
All you wanted was surface level
I needed more than that.
You quickly made an excuse
about needing to be somewhere and left.
I sat there alone thinking about what to do.
You didn't know this but I don't think we'll see each other again.
When you're gone I'm free.
I'm giving myself the freedom to let go.

Amy Littleford

Winter's Beach...

It's here,
Where I lost you,
And here,
Where I look for you still...

Shattered pieces scattered
Bu the wind and the waves,
Sharp, jagged edges
Of pain and fear,
And white-hot grief
Worn smooth.

Pieces of a girl I once knew,
Claimed by the time and the tides.

So on a Winter's beach I wander,
For its here where I lost you,
And here where I find you still...

Sunlight and Shadows

Winter's End...

My mind
has already made
its pivot
into Spring.
Now I wait
on frost-garnished
feet, with bright
green patience
in my eyes,
under these
indigo skies,
for the season
to arrive.

Garrett Ashe

Words I Wanted To Say...

Under a dark starlit sky a land of forgotten days now lie
A full moon light reveals a rocky path in reply
Down the ravines past towering sentinels of evergreen
Ancient mythic words of creation scream with wonder
Whispers on the wind of poetry I cannot comprehend
For now she stands and knocks on heaven's door

Swaying to the rhythm of the kingdom to come
My heart beat drums as my tongue dances behind my lips
A vision of you in silent beauty rises like an eclipse
My soul it craves the love I feel now escaping in waves
My mind betrayed as you turned and quietly walked away
To hear you speak the truth while believing the critique
No regrets, o'me, o'my life... nay

There are still so many words I wanted to say
The memories remain as the Lord directs the steps of man
What once tore me apart was part of a greater plan
They will see me rise in renewed strength from the darkness
Believing I am now on my own path although less traveled
There are promises to keep and miles before my final sleep
My broken heart heals as I learn how to love myself
For a higher grace is making me brand new

Mark Wayne

Year of Untangling...

To my year of tangled yarn,
Year of twisted bike chain at the park,
Year of melted chocolate on my favorite red sweater,
Year after chocolate feast on the couch with my new lover.

To my banged and bruised year,
My tissues used year –
Piled high against the wall
like a monument of surrender.

Surrender
is what I begged for –
Escape
from you, year.

Year of "When it rains it pours,"
"When door closes another one opens."
Silver linings on rain clouds filled like bile in my mouth.
I spit them out and swallowed gulps of air to keep breathing,
Seething, at you, year.

I'd never been so glad to see December.

-

It's November.

The pile of tissues have made their way to the wastebasket.

My red sweater, freshly cleaned,
brings out the copper in my concentrated eyes.

Hapless strings of multicolored yarn
stretch comfortably on my bedroom floor.

Each untangled arm reaches back
to a small sphere in my lap.

I am humming.

I don't realize I am humming,
but as I pull each inch of contorted mess into neat lines,
I am content.

Tangled yarn year, twisted chains year
Year of nearly ruined sweaters,
I promise to remember you better.
Grant you your honor due:

Year of patience, year of cleansing,
Year of untangling

Melissa Felson

Index

Ambica Gossain	Pages:	8, 52, 54, 90, 93, 122
Amy Littleford	Pages:	85, 119, 136,
Angela Marie Niemiec	Pages:	15, 33, 35, 131
Bearded Writer	Pages:	57-59
Bianca van der Kamp	Pages:	64, 91, 94, 98
Bonnie Shor	Pages:	123
Cyra Felber	Pages:	31, 48, 110
Denise Rusley	Pages:	49
Elizabeth Todoroska	Pages:	30
Emily Neuharth	Pages:	100-101, 102-103
Garrett Ashe	Pages:	27, 51, 82, 138
Geninne Woods	Pages:	24
Gina Sares	Pages:	14, 16, 81, 88, 118
Greg Oman	Pages:	26, 50, 106, 116, 126
Itchy Brained	Pages:	46, 78, 80,
Jasmine Barrett	Pages:	117
Jason Whitt	Pages:	32, 38, 60, 67
Jesselyne Abel	Pages:	55, 89, 95
Khalisa Jiwa Mawji	Pages:	56, 69, 132
Kimberly Olivera Lainez	Pages:	1, 17, 70, 71, 127
Linda Lokhee	Pages:	2-3, 20, 81, 87, 120
Lizzy in Words	Pages:	4, 10, 22, 39, 45, 47, 62, 66, 92, 107, 124, 128
Mark Wayne	Pages:	65, 84, 86, 130, 139
Melissa Felson	Pages:	6, 23, 53, 61, 63, 75, 108-109, 111, 112, 113, 115, 125, 141
Miriam Otto	Pages:	7, 28
Molly Gentzsch	Pages:	97

Nicole Carlyon   Pages: 11, 12, 18, 19, 21, 29, 36,
                                 37, 40, 41, 42, 44, 72,
                                 73, 74, 83, 105, 129

Sharmila Maitra   Pages: 43, 133-135
Steve Zmijewski   Pages: 68, 121
Sunlight and Shadows   Pages: 137
Swell Versed   Pages: 104, 114
Victoria Oliver   Pages: 34, 76, 79

To keep up to date with your favorite writers, please look for them on their Instagram accounts:

Ambica Gossain	@tryst_with_fiction
Amy Littleford	@amylittleford.author
Angela Marie Niemiec	@angel_writer
Bearded Writer	@beardedwriter_
Bianca Van Der Kamp	@vanderkampnl
Bonney Shor	@bleeshor
Cyra Felber	@herpoetrykingdom
Denise Rusley	@nobullheart
Elizabeth Todoroska	@tipsyloveletters
Emily Neuharth	@emerinn
Garrett Ashe	@garrett.ashe_
Geninne Woods	@poetrybygeninnewoods
Gina Sares	@laluzpoetry
Greg Oman	@greg.oman
Itchy Brained	@itchy_brained
Jasmine Barrett	@jasxbarrett
Jason Whitt	@jasonwhittauthor
Jesselyne Abel	@ink.jess
Khalisa Jiwa Mawji	@Khalisa_jmawji
Kimberly Olivera Lainez	@k.olivera.poetry/ kimberlyalysha_
Linda Lokhee	@lindalokheeauthor
Lizzy In Words	@lizzyinwords
Mark Wayne	@mwschutter
Melissa Felson	@intotheminefields
Miriam Otto	@miriamo77
Molly Gentzsch	@themusingsofmollymaven
Nicole Carlyon	@nicolecarlyon

Sharmila Maitra	@bonnie_maitra
Steve Zmijewski	@catchstevez
Sunlight And Shadows	@sfl_sunlightandshadows
Swell Versed	@swellversed
Victoria Oliver	@word_awakening

www.ingramcontent.com/pod-product-compliance
Lightning Source LLC
Chambersburg PA
CBHW051951170626
46808CB00007B/2564